Summary of

Leaders Eat Last

Why Some Teams Pull Together and Others Don't

by Simon Sinek

Instaread

Please Note

This is a summary with analysis.

Table of Contents

Overview

Leaders Eat Last by Simon Sinek advocates for a leadership style that focuses on serving others rather than pursuing shareholder goals or personal interests. Modern trends in leadership prioritize profits and executive bonuses over creating a healthy environment for employees. Leaders who think of themselves as serving their employees like family can increase job satisfaction and engagement, which reduces stress and increases productivity because employees feel secure. For example, in the US Marine Corps, the lowest-ranking soldiers eat first and the leaders eat last to ensure that everyone gets a chance to eat and feel cared for.

The best leaders create a Circle of Safety that encompasses the entire company, which employees can extend to the customers they serve. Poor leaders extend that Circle of Safety only to their immediate supporters, which increases stress for those outside the circle who may believe that their jobs are not secure. Good leaders avoid abstracting the people who should be inside the Circle of Safety into statistics that reflect their performance. They do so by prioritizing real interactions that involve investments of time and energy, by helping employees understand the impact of their work, and by preserving small communities where everyone knows one other.

The basis of hierarchy in human communities derives from the evolutionary advantage of living in cooperation with leaders who receive more resources in exchange for their direction. On a biological level, hormones in the human body regulate interactions and goal-seeking. Dopamine and endorphins motivate personal achievement and pain tolerance while serotonin and oxytocin create the sensation of pride and affection between people. A healthy work environment encourages a balance of these hormones, but people can develop an addiction to the short-term high from selfish hormones, such as cortisol. This type of addiction may be triggered by social media and tends to inhibit selfless behavior.

A corporate culture must support sharing ideas, learning from mistakes, integrity, and introspection in leadership. Leaders who have a strong Circle of Safety for all of their employees can entrust authority for decisions and rule-bending to the employees who are closest to the information about those decisions.

Changes in leadership philosophy over the past decades derive from the shift of leadership positions from members of the World War II generation who place a high priority on service, to Baby Boomers who have been taught to be more self-interested. The ramifications have altered political interactions in the United States as well as the national economy. The new generation taking on leadership positions may be less selfish, but is unlikely to be as selfless as those who lived through World War II.

Important People

Simon Sinek is an adjunct staff member for the Rand Corporation. He wrote the bestseller *Start With Why* (2009).

Bob Chapman is the chief executive officer and chairman of Barry-Wehmiller Companies, Inc. He advocates for service-based leadership on the Truly Human Leadership blog.

Mike Drowley is commandant at the US Air Force Weapons School. Throughout his career, he has exercised leadership that risked his personal safety for troops on his missions.

Milton Friedman (1912-2006) was a Nobel Prize-winning economist who promoted definitions of economics that emphasize selfish decisions.

Key Takeaways

✗1. Leaders should serve their employees above the company's profit margins or their selfish interests. Good leadership models resemble a supportive family.

✗ 2. A good leader interacts in person with employees, gives them a clear image of who they are helping, and invests both time and energy in them.

✗ 3. Good leaders include all employees in a Circle of Safety where they do not fear for their jobs. Employees expand that circle to customers.

✗4. Leadership hierarchies originally derived from the evolution of human communities. People have an evolutionary imperative to cooperate and give leaders more respect.

5. Human hormones incentivize both personal achievement and cooperation when they are in balance. When they are imbalanced, people may become addicted to short-term selfish gains.

✗6. People in unhealthy work environments experience high levels of stress, which has long-term health implications. Less stressed, more satisfied employees are more productive and engaged.

7. A healthy corporate culture that can survive economic trouble encourages employees to

share ideas and learn from failure. It values integrity above all else.

8. Good corporate policy avoids layoffs intended to improve profit margins because layoffs increase employees' stress and decrease their willingness to cooperate with each other.

9. Leaders must demonstrate a clear vision for employees and then entrust employees closest to the information with authority to make decisions. Employees must be allowed to bend rules.

10. The World War II generation is known for its emphasis on serving others, but Baby Boomers are more self-interested in general. Generations X and Y tend to be self-interested and prefer to deal with abstractions.

11. The structure of bonuses and work tasks in the modern workplace, as well as digital and social media, can encourage addictions to the selfish hormones at the expense of motivation to selfless actions.

12. Actions driven by selfish behavior in current leadership have resulted in deep dysfunctions in politics and the economy. Selfless behavior is exemplified in rare examples that represent ideals for the future.

Thank you for purchasing this Instaread book

**Download the Instaread mobile app to get
unlimited text & audio summaries
of bestselling books.**

Visit Instaread.co
to learn more.

Analysis

Key Takeaway 1

Leaders should serve their employees above the company's profit margins or their selfish interests. Good leadership models resemble a supportive family.

Analysis

The best leaders sacrifice money or their own interests for the interests of their followers. One model for this relationship is the leader who behaves like a parent. A good mother or father would not sacrifice a child for personal benefit and accepts responsibility for their children's safety.

One sure way to determine whether a workplace treats employees with as much consideration as family members is to look at the family leave benefits provided to workers. The United States, unlike many advanced countries, has limited provisions from state to state for paid leave when workers experience important family developments, such as the birth or adoption of a child. When employers do not offer extra paid leave for these events, parents can feel pressured to return to work as soon as possible and leave the new child with the other parent or in childcare. [1] Allowing employees to dedicate the amount of time they need to their families is one way to reduce their stress at work, have a healthier work-life balance, and ensure that they feel that their jobs are secure even though they have obligations outside the office. A leader who values strong interpersonal relationships and selfless actions would place the need for stress-free employees over the impact to the bottom line of getting every possible hour of work out of them. Such a leader would therefore accommodate adequate family leave at vital moments in employees' lives.

Key Takeaway 2

A good leader interacts in person with employees, gives them a clear image of who they are helping, and invests both time and energy in them.

Analysis

A company leader might be tempted to think of employees as numbers because many business operations depend on data. Moreover, the digital nature of many interactions might prevent leaders from engaging with employees face-to-face. If leaders think of employees as abstract numbers, they might not consider the impact of poor treatment on employees or the company's culture. A leader can avoid the inclination to think of employees as abstractions by having real interactions with them and showing them who they are helping. Leaders must invest time and energy to gain trust but must be patient with employees who are slower to trust them. Teams are best able to resist abstraction when they are small enough for everyone to know everyone else.

Since 1999, Goldman Sachs Group, Inc. has become an example of how not to treat employees, although recent developments indicate that the company may be improving in its abstraction of employees. Goldman began using layoffs to compensate for losses in the early 1990s, and it still engages in the practice. For example, 1,700 people were let go in July 2016. [2] This practice encourages employees to believe their jobs are not secure.

Goldman announced in May 2016 that it would cease to use an employee-ranking performance review and replace it with a continuous feedback system that allows the employee to actively participate. In doing so, Goldman follows the lead of many other companies that are doing away with standard performance reviews in favor of systems that provide more individual direction and encourage engagement. [3] The traditional performance review is administered by managers who quantify employees according to a rubric and store that information for review on an annual basis. This practice abstracts employees far more than a one-on-one meeting in which the manager can invest time and energy in the employee. To be most effective, one-on-one meetings should be held consistently over time and would necessitate working in small teams.

Key Takeaway 3

Good leaders include all employees in a Circle of Safety where they do not fear for their jobs. Employees expand that Circle to customers.

Analysis

In a typical corporate bureaucracy, leaders protect only those people who support them. By contrast, a good leader protects everyone so that no employees are worried about losing their job arbitrarily. When employees feel protected, they can in turn make customers feel safe.

The Circle of Safety is essential to life-saving professions, such as firefighting and internal surgery. If a surgeon doesn't include her surgical assistants in her Circle of Safety, she may end up intimidating them and thereby creating an environment in which escalated tensions and stress lead to mistakes that might not otherwise occur. For instance, a surgical assistant might not have the confidence to ask the surgeon to repeat herself when she is unclear with her instructions; this could lead to a catastrophic misunderstanding with potentially lethal and career-ending consequences. If a firefighter rushes into a smoke-filled burning building to rescue a family of five stranded on the fifth floor, he might need to rely on the other members of his company to follow him in order to make sure that both he and the victims make it out of the building alive. If the other members of his fire company have cause to distrust him, perhaps because he never praises their work or because he takes unnecessary, swashbuckling risks to show off his valiance to their chief, they might not feel comfortable taking risks on his behalf when in the midst of a challenging rescue. But even in non-life-or-death situations, the Circle of Safety is crucial for creating high-functioning work environments.

Key Takeaway 4

Leadership hierarchies originally derived from the evolution of human communities. People have an evolutionary imperative to cooperate and give leaders more respect.

Analysis

Humans have a biological mechanism that makes them feel safer in a community setting. As humans formed hunter-gatherer communities, they needed to create order to ensure everyone received needed resources. Powerful community members were given rewards to make decisions, and they ensured that others in the community received what they needed.

Later, in ancient civilizations, that hierarchy was generally difficult to escape or change. Once people were in a particular social class, classified by the income or resources they received for the work they performed, they would struggle to attain a higher status. In a civilization with effective leadership structures that create a sense of safety and stability, other markers of civilization, such as population growth, written language refinement, and styles of art, can develop. In unstable civilizations or those at war, the development of these other characteristics will suffer as people avoid relying on each other or are too occupied with survival to consider intellectual pursuits. [4]

Key Takeaway 5

Human hormones incentivize both personal achievement and cooperation when they are in balance. When they are imbalanced, people may become addicted to short-term selfish gains.

Analysis

Hormones drive human achievement and cooperation. Endorphins make people feel good about accomplishments, and dopamine gives them more resistance to pain. Serotonin makes people feel good about receiving respect, and oxytocin generates feelings of love when people interact positively. In proper balance, these hormones motivate cooperation, but too much of the selfish hormones can hinder motivation to behave selflessly.

In a given day, different people feel the effects of these hormones differently in response to the same stimuli starting with the alarm clock. If a woman feels good about waking up, begins her day with a workout, and has enough time to prepare for the day, she can expect to start the workday with a rush of endorphins that energize her. Someone whose morning is not as productive will feel less impact from endorphins and more impact from stress-related hormones, which have an effect on the ability to cope with challenges and inconveniences throughout the day. People who have a supportive family or network of friends at work will receive constant boosts of mood-improving serotonin and oxytocin, which can result in biological benefits like improved cardiovascular function and bone strength. Someone who eschews interpersonal interactions to go on smoking breaks or play non-social video games will generate more selfish hormones and reinforce a dependence that makes acquiring hormonal benefits from accomplishments like early morning workouts even less appealing. This, in turn, will lead to additional losses of potential improvements in heart health resulting from serotonin and oxytocin. [5]

Key Takeaway 6

People in unhealthy work environments experience high levels of stress, which has long-term health implications. Less stressed, more satisfied employees are more productive and engaged.

Analysis

When people are worried about personal survival or security in a work environment, they receive an excess of the hormone cortisol, which has long-term health ramifications that can shorten life spans. Stressed employees do not cooperate because they are too focused on personal interests. Employees who are not worried about their job security are more likely to cooperate.

Some employers seek other methods of lowering employee stress, although they are not always related to improving the corporate culture. One trend is the increasing establishment of meditation programs, which are intended to decrease employees' stress levels, improve their focus on goals, and inspire them to be creative. [6] Corporate yoga programs aim to improve employee health at the same time they provide outlets for stress. [7] However, if employees do not feel safe in their work spaces and are always concerned about their job security, the decreased stress levels from meditation or yoga programs would only be a short-term remedy for a long-term problem that will continue to undermine productivity and teamwork. Moreover, employees who feel unsafe at work might not feel truly at liberty to take advantage of a yoga program, even if one were offered to them.

Key Takeaway 7

A healthy corporate culture that can survive economic trouble encourages employees to share ideas and learn from failure. It values integrity above all else.

Analysis

Good leaders recognize that they can be the inspiration for positive culture change or they can be the reason the workplace culture failed its employees. Companies with strong cultures and a focus on serving employees can survive economic downturns because employees accept that everyone may need to make sacrifices to ensure that they all survive. A leader must be honest in order to cultivate the trust that is required for a strong workplace culture.

More than ever before, CEOs of large multinational corporations have enormous populations to please and impress in order to keep their jobs. These populations include employees, shareholders, regulators, industry analysts, and customers. Few people will ever have that many people counting on them to succeed and watching them when they fail, so it should be little wonder that executives can be resistant to the notion of integrity and transparency that forces them to display humility or admit mistakes. However, an executive can exert a positive impact on all of these spectators by demonstrating the cultural leadership that inspires others. Beyond demonstrating the value of selflessness for employees and shareholders, a good leader can represent a gold standard for leadership across the industry and become the ideal against which analysts measure competitors. Customers are also deeply affected by a brand's quality of leadership because their trust is easy to lose but hard to earn back if a company has been engrossed in scandal and has failed to communicate properly with consumers.

Key Takeaway 8

Good corporate policy avoids layoffs intended to improve profit margins because layoffs increase employees' stress and decrease their willingness to cooperate with each other.

Analysis

Layoffs became more popular business strategies to compensate for losses starting in the 1980s, even though they immediately made employees more concerned about their job security. When employees are too worried about their job prospects, they may act selfishly or sabotage each other to protect themselves.

Today, companies announce layoffs in every quarter and across every industry, and the rate at which companies engage in layoffs is an economic indicator grouped with hiring and unemployment. In September 2016, analysts announced that layoffs fell to the lowest number in three years even though almost 1.6 million employees were laid off in July 2016 alone. Nonetheless, planned layoffs and all announced layoffs were lower than usual. In earlier generations, 1.6 million people losing their jobs to layoffs in a single month would have been highly unusual because layoffs were simply not used by companies to balance their profits and losses. [8] Laying off employees in a downturn may be good for a company in the short term, but the ramifications for society are negative in the long term, so the rate of layoffs can both indicate the current state of the economy and predict some factors in the future as laid-off employees seek jobs and receive unemployment benefits.

Key Takeaway 9

Leaders must demonstrate a clear vision for employees and then entrust employees closest to the information with authority to make decisions. Employees must be allowed to bend rules.

Analysis

In most companies, leaders have the authority for making decisions even though employees are closer to the information needed to make those decisions. If a leader communicates a clear enough vision for the company's purpose to all employees, the employees can be given the authority to make those decisions instead and bend the rules when necessary.

Giving decision-making authority to employees who are closest to the information is a strategy proven to be successful in a variety of industries, according to productivity-focused author Charles Duhigg. In one case Duhigg outlined in his 2016 book, *Smarter Faster Better*, the Federal Bureau of Investigation gave a development team control over a complex and potentially expensive software project called Sentinel because the team leader promised to deliver the project ahead of time for a fraction of the projected cost. The team completed Sentinel four years ahead of schedule with a small portion of its original budget. They used production processes adapted from lean manufacturing, which were unfamiliar to the FBI at the time but which suited a software development team better than existing processes at the Bureau. Giving decision-making powers to a team with unusual processes may have been highly irregular when government bureaucracy was the norm, but doing so ensured that the team did not need to ask non-experts in technology for permission to do things that the project required. [9]

Key Takeaway 10

The World War II generation is known for its emphasis on serving others, but Baby Boomers are more self-interested in general. Generations X and Y tend to be self-interested and prefer to deal with abstractions.

Analysis

The generation that served in World War II had to exercise selfless behavior in many circumstances. As they raised the children of the Baby Boomer generation, they wanted to ensure that the Boomers felt they should not have to make sacrifices or go without anything they needed. Baby Boomers were therefore less likely to be selfless business leaders and politicians. As Boomers have raised members of Generations X and Y, they have passed on this emphasis on self-interest. The youngest generations are also most susceptible to becoming addicted to selfish interests with instant rewards.

The 2010s are a time of increasing age diversity in the workplace. Traditionalists, who are those born before 1946, are working past the age of 70 at a higher rate than any previous generation. Baby Boomers made up a majority of workers until 2015, at which point Millennials born between 1977 and 1997 became the majority generation. Soon, people born after 1997 will be joining the larger workforce. [10] This age diversity can generate tension in workplaces when members of certain generations feel unappreciated by other generations. For example, in a workplace centered on software development, older employees may have experience coding with older languages while younger employees began their programming educations with newer languages. The younger employees thus do not have the context of these older applications when they build projects but might also not have any inefficient habits left over from those historical applications.

Strategies to reduce this tension caused by age diversity include discouraging employees from generalizing about each other's generations. [11] When they are encouraged to work together and learn from each other, even the Traditionalists with their tendency toward selfless interests and Baby Boomers with more self-interest can cooperate in a healthy Circle of Safety with leaders that look out for them.

Key Takeaway 11

The structure of bonuses and work tasks in the modern workplace, as well as digital and social media, can encourage addictions to the selfish hormones at the expense of motivation to selfless actions.

Analysis

Selfless actions can actually be a remedy to addictions to selfish or self-gratifying behavior, as evidenced in surveys of drug or alcohol addicts in medical interventions. Recovering addicts are more likely to volunteer in their communities than the general public. People who have successfully entered long-term recovery are less likely to be receiving health care services or be involved in the criminal justice system. [12] For someone who is experiencing a hormonal addiction to the pursuit of monetary bonus rewards, social media interaction, or other selfish behaviors driven by endorphins and dopamine, volunteer work or a service-oriented approach to work can aid in decreasing reliance on the selfish hormones.

Key Takeaway 12

Actions driven by selfish behavior in current leadership have resulted in deep dysfunctions in politics and the economy. Selfless behavior is exemplified in rare examples that represent ideals for the future.

Analysis

As Baby Boomers gained control of major institutions in politics, banking, and broadcasting, their selfish tendencies damaged the selfless intentions of US politics and economic philosophy. Politicians repealed regulations that previously benefited the general public at the expense of the economy and environment and ceased cooperation between political parties.

Aside from some minor differences in deference to authority, a study of the different preferences for leadership found little variation in the leadership that Baby Boomers, Generation Xers, and Millennials expect. All generations place a high priority on a leader's ability to participate in the team, give the team the needed resources, lead with charisma, and be humane. [13] So regardless of generation, people want a humane leader and will feel secure in an environment where the leader is willing to make sacrifices for members of the team. As leadership with a service emphasis becomes more popular, the institutions currently struggling with toxic leadership may see long-term improvement because employees, regardless of generation, are coming to value many of the same characteristics.

Author's Style

Simon Sinek writes in a personal and character-driven style in *Leaders Eat Last*, which he describes as a "polemic" against the status quo of leadership theory. He focuses on individual people who either exemplified the ideal for service leadership or represented an example of how not to treat employees. Large portions of the text are dedicated to outlining the body of evidence supporting particular assertions. Other assertions, which appear to be Sinek's original concepts, are not supported with cited evidence. Sinek also coins his own terms, such as the phrase "destructive abundance," used to describe things he saw in his consulting work.

The book is divided into sections. Those sections are divided into parts, which each contain several chapters. It also includes diagrams in a hand-drawn style that are usually based on Venn diagrams.

Examples and quotes in the book are attributed to real people, using their full names, or to real companies. A few examples come from Sinek's personal life or the people for whom he consulted. Some examples and sources appear several times throughout the text, particularly the story of Bob Chapman and the companies where he established strong cultures. Sinek includes negative examples that name existing companies as well.

Sinek describes members of the World War II generation, the Baby Boomer generation, and Generations X and Y, with value judgments of their leadership styles based on generalizations. Sinek also discusses "our work," identifying himself and the reader as part of an employee population, just before referring to "we, the shareholders," so the intended audience is sometimes unclear. Sinek advocates particular positions on political issues, such as economic regulation and bipartisan cooperation. The text does not contain any citational apparatus that allows readers to easily connect facts cited with the sources that appear in the endnotes.

Author's Perspective

Simon Sinek is an adjunct staff member at the Rand Corporation, an independent public policy research organization. Sinek is also a leadership consultant and a public speaker. He originally planned to become a lawyer but left law school to pursue a goal he describes in his book as inspiring others to pursue their goals. His inspirations include self-help classics, such as *The 7 Habits of Highly Effective People* by Stephen Covey (1989) and *Who Moved My Cheese?* (1998) by Spencer Johnson. He is also inspired by behavioral economics authors including Malcolm Gladwell, Steven Levitt, Stephen Dubner, and Nicholas Taleb, and psychoanalyst Viktor Frankl. [14] Sinek gained popularity following a series of talks for TED conferences sponsored independently and for a TED conference sponsored by the Sapling Foundation.

~~~~ END OF INSTAREAD ~~~~

Thank you for purchasing this Instaread book

**Download the Instaread mobile app to get
unlimited text & audio summaries
of bestselling books.**

Visit Instaread.co
to learn more.

References

1. Boncy, Alexis. "Paid family leave, explained." *The Week*. August 2, 2016. Accessed September 18, 2016. http://theweek.com/articles/640279/paid-family-leave-explained

2. Gandel, Stephen. "Goldman Sachs Announces Its Biggest Layoffs Since Financial Crisis." *Fortune*. July 19, 2016. Accessed September 18, 2016. http://fortune.com/2016/07/19/goldman-sachs-layoffs-3/

3. Gellman, Lindsay, and Justin Baer. "Goldman Sachs to Stop Rating Employees With Numbers." *Wall Street Journal*. May 26, 2016. Accessed September 18, 2016. http://www.wsj.com/articles/goldman-sachs-dumps-employee-ranking-system-1464272443

4. Smith, Adam. *An Inquiry Into the Nature and Causes of the Wealth of Nations*. London: Methuen and Co., 1904.

5. Angier, Natalie. "Job Description Grows for Our Utility Hormone." *New York Times*. May 2, 2011. Accessed September 30, 2016. http://www.nytimes.com/2011/05/03/science/03angier.html?_r=0

6. Mueller, Elba. "5 Ways Meditation Can Benefit Businesses." *Chopra.com*. Accessed September

19, 2016. https://www.chopra.com/articles/5-ways-meditation-can-benefit-businesses

7. Elliott, David. "The benefits of yoga in the workplace." *Training Journal*. March 27, 2014. Accessed September 19, 2016. https://www.trainingjournal.com/articles/feature/benefits-yoga-workplace

8. Soergel, Andrew. "US Job Openings Hit All-Time High as Layoffs Drop to 3-Year Low." *US News & World Report*. September 7, 2016. Accessed September 19, 2016. http://www.usnews.com/news/articles/2016-09-07/us-job-openings-hit-all-time-high-as-layoffs-drop-to-3-year-low

9. Duhigg, Charles. *Smarter Faster Better: The Secrets of Being Productive in Life and Business*. New York: Random House, 2016.

10. Meister, Jeanne, and Karie Willyerd. "Are You Ready to Manage Five Generations of Workers?" *Harvard Business Review*. October 16, 2009. Accessed September 19, 2016. https://hbr.org/2009/10/are-you-ready-to-manage-five-g

11. Knight, Rebecca. "Managing People from 5 Generations." *Harvard Business Review*. September 25, 2014. Accessed September 19, 2016. https://hbr.org/2014/09/managing-people-from-5-generations

12. Harvey, Laurie. "Volunteering and working are central to addiction recovery." Sheffield Hallam University. September 22, 2015. Accessed September 19, 2016. http://www4.shu.ac.uk/mediacentre/volunteering-and-working-are-central-addiction-recovery

13. Deal, Jennifer, et al. "What Makes a Leader Effective? US Boomers, Xers, and Millennials Weigh In." Center for Creative Leadership. 2014. Accessed September 19, 2016. http://www.ccl.org/Leadership/pdf/research/WhatMakesLeaderEffective.pdf

14. Sinek, Simon. *Start With Why: How Great Leaders Inspire Everyone to Take Action.* New York: Portfolio, 2009.